FROM
GLORY
TO GLORY:
A DIVINE METAMORPHOSIS

REBECCA HARGROVE

WESTBOW
PRESS®
A DIVISION OF THOMAS NELSON
& ZONDERVAN

Scripture quotations marked (NIV) are taken from the Holy Bible, New International Version®, NIV®. Copyright © 1973, 1978, 1984, 2011 by Biblica, Inc.™ Used by permission of Zondervan. All rights reserved worldwide.

WestBow Press books may be ordered through booksellers or by contacting:

WestBow Press
A Division of Thomas Nelson & Zondervan
1663 Liberty Drive
Bloomington, IN 47403
www.westbowpress.com
1 (866) 928-1240

ISBN: 978-1-5127-6302-7 (sc)

Print information available on the last page.

WestBow Press rev. date: 12/6/2016

CONTENTS

Preface ix

Dedication xi

The Winged Life: Metamorphosis Through Transformation 1

On Redeeming Gomer--The Book of Hosea 5

An Alabaster Jar of Perfume 6

Everything is Possible. . . Mark 9:23 7

Death-Grip Depression 8

Heaven's Hope 9

Hope-Building 11

A Desolate Woman 14

The High Cost of Obedience 18

He Knows the Way 21

Shut the Door 24

Abandonment 26

The Weight of the World 28

Common Clay 30

He Will Lift You Up 32

Rejoicing In the Lord Always 34

New Every Morning 36

Like A Little Child 38

Belief is the Key 41

The Deliverer 44

Meditation versus Self-Medication 47

The Great Physician 51

A Crown of Beauty 54

A Divided Heart 57

Speck-Busters 60

Humility 62

Through the Fire 65
Busy Hands 68
Hidden Faces 71
No More Tears 73
Celebrate Survival 75
Setting Boundaries 77
Dysfunction Junction 79
The Least of These 81
How Much is Enough? 83
The Furnace of Affliction- Part One 86
The Furnace of Affliction- Part Two 89
Furnace of Affliction- Part Three 92
When the World is Upside Down 95
Balancing on Life's Tightrope 98
Winning the War 101
Enlarged Vision 103
Rejection 105
Cultivating Hope 107
Bearing with One Another 109
Human Hope Is Fragile: Dreams Fulfilled by God are Fortifying 111
Living Out Your True Identity 113
Hiding Place 115
Setting Boundaries for Sanity and Sobriety 117
Get to the Root of It 119
The Furnace 121
Giving Back 123
Letting Go To Let God 124
Myths of Mental Illness 125
Don't Give Up 126
The School of Suffering 127
The Ones We Forget 128
The Human Cost of Suffering 129
Beauty for Ashes 130
Lessons From a Butterfly 131
Detoxification 132
Battling the Winds and Waves to Heal One Man 134

Present Sufferings for Future Glory 137
The One True Hope-Giver 139
The Almighty Will Be Your Gold..141
The Glory Revealed in Us 143

PREFACE

I began writing this book ten years ago when I was staying in a long-term treatment facility for addiction. It occurred to me at that time that not much had been written for those recovering from mental illness and addiction—dual diagnosis.

I sensed that many struggling with a dual diagnosis had very little hope of recovery. The revolving door of fixing the mental illness with medication often swings back open when the self-medication of substance abuse starts once again, leaving the patient on a merry-go-round of sorts that never ends.

My 18-year journey through mental illness and my 20-year struggle with addictions have taught me several valuable lessons: 1) no one's program of treatment looks the same; 2) no one can help another human being until they're ready for help; and 3) lastly, but more importantly, the Lord Jesus Christ is the Deliverer. Programs like Celebrate Recovery and Addicts Victorious focus on the power of God to change lives, enabling us to overcome obstacles too large for any of us to surmount.

It is my hope that this collection of daily reflections and poems encourage not only those struggling with dual diagnosis but also those family and friends who want insight into how best to support their loved ones. May God bless you on your journey and give you hope through our hope-giver, the Lord Jesus Christ.

DEDICATION

This Book is Dedicated to My Mother

Who always believed in me, even when I didn't;

Who selflessly poured her life into mine;

Who treated me with dignity and respect after my diagnosis of bipolar;

Who took me in and cared for me when I couldn't take care of myself;

Who always encouraged me that my life wasn't over simply because I
    had a dual diagnosis;

Who made my dreams possible by personal sacrifice;

Who loved me when I was quite unlovable;

Who supported my abilities and gifts;

Who held my hand when I was so overmedicated, I could barely walk;

Who stayed by my bedside at the hospital when I overdosed;

Who moved me out of my apartment when I needed her support after
    a manic episode;

Who got me into a group home when it seemed there were no other
    options to keep me sober;

Who has always fought to get me the best possible medical care;

Who is my spiritual mentor and best friend;

Who exemplifies the Lord Jesus Christ to me daily.

THE WINGED LIFE: METAMORPHOSIS THROUGH TRANSFORMATION

"Now the Lord is the Spirit; and where the Spirit of the Lord is, there is liberty. But we all, with unveiled face beholding as in a mirror the glory of the Lord, are being transformed in the same image from glory to glory . . ." II Corinthians 3:17-18 NIV

"Therefore, I urge you, brothers, in view of God's mercy, to offer your bodies as living sacrifices, holy and pleasing to God--this is your spiritual act of worship. Do not conform any longer to the pattern of this world, but be transformed by the renewing of your mind. Then you will be able to test and approve what God's will is--his good, pleasing, and perfect will." Romans 12:1-2 NIV

I love butterflies. The way they float effortlessly, their magnificent beauty and varieties, and their strength while yet so fragile all impress me. But what impresses me the most is that the Creator designed butterflies to be one of only a few creatures that undergoes complete metamorphosis. From egg to larva--voracious, leaf-eating caterpillars--to the adult state--winged wonders--I marvel that the transformation is so complete. Of course, the pupa stage, or chrystalis, is where the real magic happens. Scientists are still baffled about just how that complete transformation takes place.

It seems to me there is no better illustration and comparison of the metamorphosis God wants to birth in us through salvation and overcoming addiction and mental illness than the life cycle of the butterfly. What a beautiful metaphor from nature are butterflies for those of us with

1

old habits and lives to shed! Complete metamorphosis--the spirit-filled life--is only possible through salvation in Jesus Christ. This verse in II Corinthians says that "we all . . . are being transformed" into the very image of God. Those of us who are believers are constantly in the process of being transformed, from "glory to glory", one stage of mirroring God's likeness to the next. God's ultimate goal for us as earth creatures is to glorify Him, and that simply isn't possible if we're stuck in our carnal, caterpillar state.

The caterpillar, or larva, which emerges from its egg casing on a leaf, has only one goal: to feed its flesh! It eats all the time, growing larger and larger as it eats. Interestingly enough, the bright colors of various caterpillars are produced by the toxins they ingest eating their leaves of choice. These serve as a warning sign to predators that they are poisonous.

Can you imagine if each of us wore signs warning others what our "poisons" were or how our flesh operated? My sign might read: "DANGER! Approval-seeking perfectionist with tendencies to stuff emotion, self-medicate, erupt into anger or withdraw into isolation and depression. Handle with caution!"

Of course, we humans feed our flesh in so many different ways: materialism, self-obsession, addictions from alcohol to the Internet, compulsions to overeat, shop, gamble, and buy pornographic material, and the list goes on and on . . .

It is fascinating that caterpillars, while they have colorful markings to warn possible predators, do not have good eyesight, making them largely unaware of imminent danger. That is precisely how we humans are when we are gorging our flesh in sinful desires. We become so focused and obsessed with trying to meet our deep needs with superficial fixes that we don't see the looming threat of physical and spiritual death.

"Those who live according to the sinful nature have their minds set on what that nature desires; but those who live in accordance with the Spirit have their minds set on what the Spirit desires. The mind of sinful man is death, but the mind controlled by the Spirit is life and peace. . ." Romans 8:5-6 *NIV*

God's Word tells us that the outcome of sin--feeding the flesh--is death, spiritually and physically. "For if you live according to the sinful nature, you will die; but if by the Spirit you put to death the misdeeds of the body, you will live. . ." Romans 8:13 *NIV*

Perhaps the most mysterious part of metamorphosis is what happens in the chrystalis. Scientists are still baffled by the enzymes that seem to trigger complete transformation from caterpillar to butterfly in this suspended sac of super energy.

As Christians, Christ's blood is the only atoning sacrifice that can transfer us from the kingdom of darkness to light, removing the penalty of our sin. But is is the mysterious work of the Holy Spirit that gives us the "winged life", the power and transformation from salvation to superabundant life!

The Holy Spirit is not only the seal God sets on us the day we become His child, but more importantly, He is the part of the Holy Trinity responsible for our sanctification, convicting us of sin and giving us the power to overcome. The Holy Spirit fills us with special anointings to do the work of the Lord, giving us extra measures of courage, grace, love, peace, wisdom, insight, and other kinds of talents to serve others when we need it. The Holy Spirit is our catalyst in the chrysalis of salvation, empowering life-changing work that only He can do.

We also must play a part in our transformation. Just as the caterpillar voraciously eats leaves for the transformation energy that will be needed for the complete metamorphosis, so we must voraciously read and absorb God's Word to renew our mind, according to Romans 12:2 NIV. What a wonderful promise Paul gives us here: If we renew of minds, we will be able to test and approve (know) what God's will is. We will know God and His will for us more clearly and intimately.

The glorious butterfly that emerges from the chrysalis represents the shedding of the old sin nature to live a spirit-filled life, yielded to God. The results of such a beautiful life are the fruits of the Spirit: love, joy, peace, patience, kindness, gentleness, goodness, faithfulness, and self-control. (Galatians 5:22-23 *NIV*)

"Therefore, if anyone is in Christ, he is a new creation; the old has gone, the new has come!" II Corinthians 5:17 NIV. In both mental illness and addiction, "recovery" is a slippery term, for there are aspects of our old lives that we will never wish nor be able to recover. Instead, we must focus our eyes on Jesus, allowing the Lord to work the miraculous "new creation" in us while we make daily progress.

While appearing quite delicate, butterflies are actually quite strong, migrating thousands of miles, multi-generationally, from Canada to Mexico each year, as the Monarch does. We as humans are frail also, our days on earth number only a few years, and we are gone. But God gives us superhuman strength through the Holy Spirit to face every obstacle, sorrow, suffering, and temptation we face. He longs for us to shed our caterpillar suit and be metamorphosed by the power of the Holy Spirit to live the winged life.

Salvation is the first step to the winged life. Are you ready to fly?

On Redeeming Gomer--The Book of Hosea

Bound and condemned on the auction block,
Enslaved by a life of sin;
Stripped naked of all pride and peace,
Tormented by demons within.
Her husband she'd forsaken,
Whoring after fleshly delights;
Her children cursed and abandoned,
God's mercy seemed to have taken flight.
But God's Word came to Hosea:
"Go and buy back your prostitute wife.
Take her home and gently restore her.
Mercifully redeem back her destitute life."
What a poignant picture of salvation!
On the auction block to be sold, enslaved, condemned,
Bound and shackled, we'd spent our lives a 'whoring,
While our husband Jesus Christ suffered our sin.
Enduring unspeakable humiliation,
Suffering and bleeding stripes,
He paid the full price of our redemption,
And bought for us eternal life.

AN ALABASTER JAR OF PERFUME

An act of kindness so rich and amazing,
A love offering spilt to anoint His feet;
His host, Simon, incensed by the display,
Yet Jesus, his guest, he did not kiss nor greet.
"Simon," Jesus asked, reading his thoughts,
"Which of these two men loved more?
The one forgiven a little,
or the one forgiven a great score?"
The answer was obvious,
contained in that jar;
The woman, a sinner, unclean,
Poured out her love overflowing and unmarred.
Tears from years of sin
Bathed the Master's feet;
She anointed them with perfume,
Unaware that Death he'd soon meet.
She dried His feet with her hair,
The only towel she had;
Soon He would go to the cross
To spill His blood to redeem man.
Lord, may I pour out my alabaster jar each day
Upon your feet,
As I worship and adore you,
Your merciful sacrifice I need.

EVERYTHING IS POSSIBLE. . .
MARK 9:23

A crowd was gathering around the disciples,
Ready to claim defeat,
Over the unclean spirit who'd ravished a boy;
For years there'd been no reprieve.
"O, unbelieving generation!
How long must I be with you?" Jesus exclaimed.
At the sound of Jesus' voice,
The unholy spirit tried to harm and maim.
The boy, who'd often been thrown by the demon,
Bent to destroy, "Jesus," the father said,
"If you can help us, please take pity on my boy."
"If?" said Jesus. "Everything is possible
for him who believes," the Master replied.
"Oh, help my unbelief Jesus!
I do believe!" the father cried.
Jesus commanded the demon to leave
And never to return;
The child was lifeless, appearing dead,
But Jesus helped him up, never again to be burned.
If everything is possible for him who believes,
Why aren't we claiming by faith miracles to receive?
Let us cry out, as the father did, "Jesus, help my unbelief!"
And blessings will begin that we could never conceive!

DEATH-GRIP DEPRESSION

Choking from a lack of fresh air,
Relentless reeling into despair.
Vice-grip tightens, like a noose,
Struggling yet, unable to get loose.
Overwhelmed, oppressed, worries obscure,
When the wound's this deep, who can cure?
God Almighty, have mercy on me!
Take the grave clothes I wear and set me free.
My soul, which longs to worship you still,
Unhindered, undaunted by depression's chill.
Unthaw the frozen depths, warmed by the Son,
Liquify the ice, let the waters run.
Down the peaks of my mountains, terrible and dark,
To the streams of healing, where scars no more mark.
This frail mind of mine, bathed in your Word,
Wash me, cleanse me, give me joy unheard.

HEAVEN'S HOPE

If I carry the cross of Jesus,
Hope's not a frailty or whimsical wish;
It's not luck or an outside chance of survival;
It's God's promise for plans to bless.
In Hebrews, our hope is an anchor,
Mooring us steadfastly to promises of God;
Since we know it is impossible for Him to lie,
We can enter behind the veil,
Where Christ, our High Priest, trod.
In Lamentations, the Lord is good
To those whose hope is in Him;
Because of the Lord's compassions which never fail,
Our hope is new each day and never dim.
In Jeremiah, the Lord declares plans to prosper us
And give us a hope and a future;
We will seek Him and find Him when we search with all our heart,
Making God our life's sole venture.
In Isaiah, He's the Hope-Giver
who rebukes us not to dwell on the past;
"See, I am doing a new thing!,"
Making a way through desert paths.
In Psalm 71 *NIV*, David exclaims, "But as for me, I will always have hope";
He will praise the Lord more and more;
Though He has made him see troubles,
His life again God will restore.
Is your life built upon the Solid Rock, or
Precariously-perched on sinking sand?
For hope that's unwavering,
Reach out for Jesus' hand.

"Why are you downcast, O my soul? Why so disturbed within me? Put your hope in God, for I will yet praise Him, My Savior and my God." Psalm 42:11 NIV

"Find rest, O my soul, in God alone; my hope comes from him." Psalm 62:5 NIV

"But as for me, I will always have hope; I will praise you more and more." Psalm 71:14 NIV

Hope-Building

I recently decided to help start a new monthly support group for our community's Depression Bipolar Support Alliance chapter, called "Hope-Building" for those struggling through the mire of mental illness. My new venture has spawned much research into the word, "hope", and caused me to realize how vital hope is for broken people.

The word "hope" is defined as a wish, desire, or dream that carries with it the expectation of fulfillment. This stands in stark contrast to wishes, desires, or dreams that have no expectation of fulfillment, whether they are unrealistic or simply not possible. Hope gives promise of what IS possible, and sustains us until the wish, desire, or dream is fulfilled.

How desperately we broken people need hope! It is the impetus for change, the wind in our sails, the very air we need to breathe. Hope gives us strength to follow through, the courage to dream, and even promotes mental and physical healing. Hope is the stuff that gets us out of bed in the morning to face the day.

In Psalm 65:5 *NIV*, David says that it is the Lord who is the hope of all the ends of the earth and of the farthest seas. The word "hope" is used over 25 times in the book of Psalms.

In this dark, uncertain, sin-filled world we live in, where lives are marred and broken, we desperately need hope just to survive, hope for a better day tomorrow, hope that our lives will have meaning, and that addictions and mental illness can be overcome. Jesus Christ is that Hope Giver.

"But he was pierced for our transgressions, he was crushed for our iniquities; the punishment that brought us peace was upon Him, and by his wounds we are healed." Isaiah 53:5 *NIV*.

"We have this hope as an anchor for the soul, firm and secure. It enters the inner sanctuary behind the curtain, where Jesus, who went before us, has entered on our behalf. He has become a high priest forever, in the order of Melchizedek." Hebrews 6:19-20 *NIV.*

Jesus is the hope that anchors our soul, for it is by His wounds we are healed.

I know that as long as I wear this earth suit, I will continue to struggle with crippling bouts of depression, the temptation to self-medicate, sleepless nights, and tastes of mania, but my hope lies in what Jesus accomplished on the cross--my eternal destiny in heaven. The hope of that rich inheritance and the daily reprieve of forgiveness I so desperately need to dust myself off and get back up again fills me with expectation of fulfillment.

"Hope deferred makes the heart sick, but a longing fulfilled is a tree of life." Proverbs 13:12 *NIV.*

Jesus wants to fulfill our heart's longings and be the hope that anchors our soul. Are you drifting aimlessly through unchartered waters, far off course, or is your very life moored firmly to the Rock of Ages? Christ, our Hope Builder, holds within the gale!

"Sing, O barren woman, you who never bore a child; burst into song, shout for joy, you who were never in labor; because more are the children of the desolate woman than of her who has a husband," says the Lord. . . "Do not be afraid; you will not suffer shame. Do not fear disgrace; you will not be humiliated. You will forget the shame of your youth and remember no more the reproach of your widowhood. For your Maker is your husband--the Lord Almighty is His name--the Holy One of Israel is your Redeemer; he is called the God of all the earth. The Lord will call you back as if you were a wife deserted and distressed in spirit--a wife who married young, only to be rejected," says your God. "For a brief moment I abandoned you, but with deep compassion I will bring you back . . ." Isaiah 54:1, 4-7 NIV

A Desolate Woman

I have often heard it said that the Bible is God's love letter to us as individuals, but I never grasped that concept until I was transformed by these verses in Isaiah.

Isaiah, chapter 54, according to biblical scholars, is about the future glory of Zion, when Christ returns to the earth and there is created the New Jerusalem, described in Revelation 21.

In Jewish culture, a woman who was barren carried a similar social stigma as a person with an addiction or mental illness does now. These women were outcasts, on the fringe of society, because God had not blessed their womb. The Bible speaks of children, the fruit of the womb, being the strength of a man and a reward (Psalm 127:3-5 *NIV*). Men could divorce their wives for being childless. The heartache and pain that accompanied barrenness was isolating, humiliating, and disgraceful.

A desolate place has no life, and a desolate woman has no children, her life void of one of the purposes woman was created for, childbirth and child-rearing.

But in these verses in Isaiah, God offers consolation to these women figuratively in the future of Zion. He holds out the promise that they will "not suffer shame," and "will not be humiliated, (v.4 NIV) because their "Maker is (their) husband. . ." (v. 5 *NIV*). God even promises in verse one that the desolate woman has more "children" than a woman with a husband!

I am a desolate woman. I never had any children because at the height of my childbearing years, I was battling addictions and bipolar disorder. "The shame of my youth" (v. 4 *NIV*) was the groundwork I had laid early on to use and abuse substances to feel better.

I somehow managed to hide my alcoholism from my husband in the early years of our marriage, but it eventually caught up with me. My poor husband had to deal with not only my bipolar illness, but also my addictions--it was too much for him. He finally told me to leave, and informed me that if I didn't go into a year-long treatment facility, he wanted a divorce.

I felt "deserted and distressed in spirit, a wife who married young, only to be rejected." (v. 6 *NIV*). With deep compassion, God has "called me back" over the last 15 years. Through myriads of treatment centers, psych units, group homes, battles with self-medication, and the stigma of mental illness and addiction, God has proven to me that His kindness is everlasting (v. 8 *NIV*).

God, in His severe mercies, did not bless me with biological children. I'm confident He knew I was neither mentally or physically capable of raising them. However, He has instead blessed me with other "children": my niece and nephews, who fill my heart with joy, and others I have helped "mother", providing support and strength that I wouldn't have been able to give if I had been raising my own children.

"'Though the mountains be shaken and the hills be removed, yet my unfailing love for you will not be shaken, nor my covenant of peace be removed,' says the Lord, who has compassion on you." - Isaiah 54:10 *NIV*

NOTES

"During the days of Jesus' life on earth, he offered up prayers and petitions with loud cries and tears to the one who could save him from death, and he was heard because of his reverent submission. Although he was a son, he learned obedience from what he suffered. . ." Hebrews 5:7-8 NIV

THE HIGH COST OF OBEDIENCE

We cherish the things we pay a high price for. The freedoms Americans desperately cling to were bought at the high cost of human life. Antiquities and famous artworks are auctioned off to the highest bidder, bottles of fine, rare wine are sold for more than most of us make in a month, and the automobiles we cherish leave us with car payments that a Filipino family of eight could live off of for a year! I admit that I pay a dear price for my cable TV every month just to have 125 channels to choose from, a fact I'm not proud of. The bottom line is we're willing to pay a high price for the things we value.

Now, survey the high cost you've paid in life for addictions and/or mental illness--doctors, counselors, hospitals, therapy, prescriptions, rehabs, jails, lost self-esteem, lost checks, lost jobs, lost relationships, lost peace of mind, lost time, lost opportunities, shattered dreams--the cost is very high. We've paid dearly, and we were willing to pay the price to chase the elusive "cure", the next fix, anything to diminish our suffering even if the reprieve was short-lived.

It must grieve God so deeply to see the lengths we humans will go to to relieve suffering. Yet, the School of Suffering seems to be the alma mater of choice to teach humans obedience. That's a painful pill to swallow.

Verse 8 in this Hebrews passage tells us that although Jesus Christ was the very Son of God, Deity Incarnate, "he learned obedience from what he suffered." If the Son of God himself had to learn obedience during his stay on earth, how much more do we frail humans need to learn in this manner?

Jesus Christ's obedience to God cost Him everything--his death on the cross as the Savior of our souls demanded he willingly lay down his life, suffer unspeakable torture, and for a brief moment in human history, God turned his back on Him, unable to look upon the full weight of sin debt from mankind. In those hours of physical agony on the cross, Christ suffered separation from God the Father, crying out in a loud voice, "My God, my God, why have you forsaken me?" (Mark 15:34 *NIV*). That abandonment was far worse than the physical pain. Yet, Christ learned the high cost of obedience and willingly did it for us!

I believe God allows suffering in our lives to conform us to His image--to teach us obedience. The suffering can make us bitter or better--the choice is ours.

"But he knows the way that I take; when he has tested me, I will come forth as gold." Job 23:10 NIV

". . . When you see a (spiritual) giant, remember the road you must travel to come up to his side is not along the sunny lane where wildflowers ever bloom; but a steep, rocky, narrow pathway where the blasts of hell will almost blow you off your feet; where the sharp rocks cut the flesh, where the projecting thorns scratch the brow, and the venomous beasts hiss on every side." (E.A. Kilbourne, in <u>Streams in the Desert</u>, Mrs. Charles E. Cowman, Zondervan Publishing House, 1925, p. 220.)

HE KNOWS THE WAY

More than any other man in the Bible, with the one exception of the Lord Jesus Christ himself, Job experienced deep, profound suffering and mental anguish. He stands as the symbol of tragedy, with the entire book's theme, "Why do bad things happen to good people?" as resoundingly - familiar today as it was in 2000 B.C.

Job's suffering was so apparent to his three friends who come to console him that they hardly recognized him (chap. 2, v. 12 *NIV*), his pain so raw and pervasive. They began "to weep aloud, and they tore their robes and sprinkled dust on their heads. Then they sat on the ground with him for seven days and seven nights. No one said a word to him, because they saw how great his suffering was." (Job 2:12-13 *NIV*).

Why would God have allowed Satan to test Job in this way? It is an age-old question that only God knows the answer to. The Bible says that Job was "blameless and upright; he feared God and shunned evil." (Job 1:1 *NIV*) His wife, overwhelmed by the tragic losses, tells her husband to "Curse God and die" (Job 1:9 *NIV*). But Job replies to her, "You are talking like a foolish woman. Shall we accept good from God and not trouble?" (Job 2:10 *NIV*). Job trusted that God "knew the way," regardless of how desperate his circumstances were. He trusted that his faith in God, though tested in the fires of affliction, would "come forth as gold." (Job 23:10 *NIV*). "Though he slay me, yet will I hope in him", . . . (Job 13:15 *NIV*).

Those of us who struggle with depression, schizophrenia, bipolar disorder, or anxiety, have asked God countless times, "Why me?" Our vain attempts to mask the pain only served to increase and intensify our suffering.

"Does not man have hard service on earth? Are not his days like those of a hired man? Like a slave longing for the evening shadows, or a hired man waiting eagerly for his wages, so I have been allotted months of futility, and nights of misery have been assigned to me. When I lie down, I think, 'How long before I get up?' The night drags on, and I toss till dawn. My body is clothed with worms and scabs, my skin is broken and festering. My days are swifter than a weaver's shuttle, and they come to an end without hope. Remember, O God, that my life is but a breath; my eyes will never see happiness again. The eye that now sees me will see me no longer; you will look for me, but I will be no more. . .When I think my bed will comfort me and my couch will ease my complaint, even then you frighten me with dreams and terrify me with visions, so that I prefer strangling and death, rather than this body of mine. I despise my life; I would not live forever. Let me alone; my days have no meaning." Job 7:1-8, 13-16 *NIV.*

Though the dark night of the soul may seem unending, the path of our life buffeted by the fiery blasts of hell itself, God Almighty knows the way. In that, we may cling to Him to carry us through.

"Forget the former things; do not dwell on the past. See, I am doing a new thing! Now it springs up; do you not perceive it? I am making a way in the desert and streams in the wasteland." Isaiah 43:18-19 NIV

"But one thing I do: Forgetting what is behind and straining toward what is ahead, I press on toward the goal to win the prize for which God has called me heavenward in Christ Jesus." Philippians 3:13-14 NIV.

Shut the Door

"When one door closes another opens. But we often look so long and so regretfully upon the closed door that we fail to see the one that has opened for us." - Helen Keller

When we survey the wreckage of our past lives, there is a temptation to look back so longingly at the closed doors that we fail to see those now open.

In the wake of my descent into mental illness and addiction, I saw doors close on my marriage, my independence, my finances, my career, my future possibilities.

I'm so grateful that God is a door opener: "I am doing a new thing! Now it springs up; do you not perceive it?" Isaiah 43:19 *NIV.* God, in His infinite mercy, never closes one door without opening another. We must choose to shut the door on the past and walk through the doors of our future. We must, as Paul states, " press on toward the goal to win the prize for which God has called me heavenward in Christ Jesus." Philippians 3:14 *NIV.*

The Big Book of Alcoholics Anonymous states that in our recovery, we will not regret the past nor wish to close the door on it. But I believe God insists in these verses that we say goodbye to where we've been in order to move on to what He has in store. He is "making a way in (our) desert and streams in the wasteland (of our past and present!)" - Isaiah 43:19 *NIV*

A Danny Gokey song, "Tell Your Heart to Beat Again", from his album, Hope In Front of Me, states: "Yesterday's a closing door--you don't live there anymore. Say goodbye to where you've been and tell your heart to beat again."

Put your hand on the doorknob of the past and quietly shut the door. You don't live there anymore, and God wants you to step through the threshold of your future.

> *"For a brief moment I abandoned you, but with deep compassion I will bring you back. In a surge of anger I hid my face from you for a moment, but with everlasting kindness I will have compassion on you,'says the Lord your Redeemer." - - Isaiah 54:7-8 NIV*

ABANDONMENT

Perhaps when you were a child, you got a frightening taste of being left behind by your family. You slipped away from your mother or father's grasp for a moment, and the next instance, you realized you couldn't locate them. Whether in a crowded department store or large public event, you panicked as you frantically began looking for them. You cried, got the attention of some adults, and were so relieved when you were finally reunited. . .

The emotional and/or physical abandonment some of us experienced as a child scarred us for life. This root of rejection is so primal and painful that we wince today when we think of it. In my own experience, I can trace very poor self-esteem, approval-seeking behavior, and oversensitivity to criticism/perceived rejection all from emotional abandonment. Such a poor foundation leaves cracks and fissures so deep that the 'elements' can destroy: peer pressure, self-medication, rebellion, isolation, deep-seated resentments, self-destructive behaviors, compulsivity. . . the list goes on and on.

Thank God that He never turns His back on us! He will never leave us nor forsake us. Even after the nation of Israel's idolatry, forsaking their first love, and blatant disregard of all the Lord had done for them, the Lord still had compassion on them and promised to bring them back (v. 7 NIV). His abandonment was brief, allowing the nation of Israel to go into captivity because of the hardness of their hearts.

Allow the Lord your God to help you forgive those who have abandoned you, heal the painful scars, and rejoice that the Lord Jesus never forsakes us! We are his eternally.

"Why are you downcast, O my soul? Why so disturbed within me? Put your hope in God, for I will yet praise Him, my Savior and my God." Psalm 42:11 NIV

THE WEIGHT OF THE WORLD

Depression is a debilitating and mysterious disease. It seems that some days, no matter how hard I try to do all the right things to stay "UP", I'm destined to be "DOWN".

I can rise early, spend quiet time reading my Bible and devotional books, praying, take all of my medications, exercise for an hour, talk to loved ones on the phone, and yet this FUNK persists. It feels like the weight of the world is resting squarely on my shoulders, and no matter what I do, it persists.

It is on days like these that I must thank and praise God for the smallest of victories and the most mundane aspects of life that I take for granted.

"Thank you Lord for my air conditioner in this 108-degree weather. Thank you Lord for enough good food to eat in my kitchen. Thank you Lord for medicine that keeps my thinking clear and sane."

Counting my blessings forces me to acknowledge all the good things in my life that are from God. When I focus on these things, the feelings of despair lift and I realize how much I have to be thankful for.

COMPLICITY

> *"But who are you, O man, to talk back to God? Shall what is formed say to him who formed it, 'Why did you make me like this?' Does not the potter have the right to make out of the same lump of clay some pottery for noble purposes and some for common use?"* - Romans 9:20-21 NIV

COMMON CLAY

Being afflicted with a mental illness and an addictive personality, with the overwhelming desire to self-medicate, left me shaking my fist at God. "Why did you make me like this?!" has become a desperate, frequent cry of mine to God.

The bottom line is, however, that God is the Potter and He gets to mold the clay anyway He sees fit. God gets to be God. Would I have chosen an easier, softer way if given the chance? Of course I would have. But His purposes and ways are higher than my ways, and one of His sole purposes while forming me on His potter's wheel is to conform me to the image of Christ.

When I was in my mid-twenties, I earned a bachelor's degree, graduating cum laude. I then went on to earn a master's degree in Teaching English As a Second Language, convinced that God had some noble calling on my life to travel overseas and be a tentmaker, sharing the Gospel with those students of other faiths. But my bipolar illness and addiction prevented that, and I became despondent that God wanted me for a common use rather than a noble purpose.

David in Psalms 84:10 *NIV* says that he would "rather be a doorkeeper in the house of my God than dwell in the tents of the wicked."

I too am now content to be a lowly "doorkeeper", for the Lord knew that if I had had a more stressful, prestigious calling, I might have fallen into pride, wickedness, and more severe mental illness and addiction. Thank the Lord that He safeguards the simpleminded.

"God opposes the proud but gives grace to the humble. Submit yourselves, then, to God. Resist the devil, and he will flee from you. Come near to God and he will come near to you. Wash your hands, you sinners, and purify your hearts, you double-minded. Grieve, mourn, and wail. Change your laughter to mourning and your joy to gloom. Humble yourselves before the Lord, and he will lift you up." --James 4:6b-10 NIV

HE WILL LIFT YOU UP

Before my mental breakdown, I was a proud person. I was proud about my upper-middle class upbringing and the lifestyle it afforded. I was proud that I graduated cum laude of my journalism class, and I was really proud that I graduated with my master's degree with a 4.0 grade point average. After climbing the dizzying heights to reach the pinnacle of my academic career, I tumbled down the mountain of pride to land at the bottom with a mental diagnosis and addiction diagnosis. I had come face to face with true humility, as dual diagnosis is a great equalizer; mental illness and addiction don't discriminate based on your income, education, or race.

When we are proud, we feel we really don't need God. Oh, we may relegate him to our back pocket, retrieving him on occasion when it is fitting. But it is in true humility that we sense our utter and desperate need for Him, that we seek to draw near Him because of our utter depravity.

Our utter depravity in the presence of a pure, holy God should drive us, as these verses in James point out, to grieve, mourn, and wail over our sin--to mourn and be gloomy over our weaknesses. For it is when we experience our dependence on Christ's salvation through forgiveness of sin, God can lift us up. He will give us grace to handle our weaknesses.

"Though the fig tree does not bud and there are no grapes on the vine, though the olive crop fails and the fields produce no food, though there are no sheep in the pen and no cattle in the stalls, yet I will rejoice in the Lord, I will be joyful in God my Savior." --Habakkuk 3:17-18 NIV

Rejoicing In the Lord Always

It's easy to be thankful to the Lord when our outward circumstances are pleasing. . . our job is going well, we have the creature comforts to enjoy life, our family relations are good, and our finances are in order.

However, when we find ourselves without a job, ekking out a living on disability, family relations frought with tension, and our finances in sorry shape, it is difficult to rejoice in God our Savior.

In any given moment in our lives, it is not our outward circumstances that define us, though we are sorely tested to let them control us. Instead, we need to understand that God allows adversity in our lives to conform us to the likeness of Jesus. Our heavenly Father wants us to focus on Him and the goodness in our lives He brings and not on outward circumstances. Those passing circumstances are temporary, while God in His infinite mercy never changes.

Paul tells us to "Rejoice in the Lord always. I will say it again "Rejoice!" --Phillipians 4:4 *NIV*. No life circumstances can ever separate us from God's love: "For I am convinced that neither death nor life, neither angels nor demons, neither the present nor the future, nor any powers, neither height nor depth nor anything else in all creation, will be able to separate us from the love of God that is in Christ Jesus our Lord."--Romans 8:38-39 *NIV*

"Because of the Lord's great love we are not consumed, for His compassions never fail. They are new every morning; great is your faithfulness." Lamentations 3:22-23 NIV

NEW EVERY MORNING

In my active addiction to alcohol and bouts of crippling depression, there was a weighty dread to each day when I opened my eyes. It seemed like I was walking in cement shoes, enduring the pain of my insanity of doing the same things over and over again, expecting different results. Of course. the results were always the same, and I'd dread tomorrow when I'd get up and do it all over again.

I've heard that a rut is an early grave you dig yourself. God never intended us to wake up dreading the day. If you do, your perspective and actions probably need changing. And God is in the business of change.

That's why worship and praising God are essential, as well as prayer. These forms of adoration are intended not to change or manipulate God, who never waivers or changes, but to change us--our attitudes of the heart.

Every morning that you open your eyes, God has new compassions--acts of love and kindness--that He wants to bestow on you, new grace to handle the life issues of the day. Will you chose to praise Him in spite of your limitations and specific circumstances? Will you accept your lot in life from Him, even if it didn't turn out quite the way you'd planned?

He gives us a clean slate each day. Will you choose to praise Him for His faithfulness to you today?

"I tell you the truth; anyone who will not receive the Kingdom of God like a little child will never enter it." Mark 10:15 NIV

LIKE A LITTLE CHILD

My father, whom I love and appreciate more each day, has confounded me frequently by telling me that my mental illness makes me child-like. The underlying message from him is that my thinking and judgment are sometimes, well . . . infantile. Bipolar disorder, especially unmedicated, leads to some disordered thinking and impulsive behavior. But I also believe the illness, in some degree or measure, returns us to a state of simple trust and faith, where we are forced to rely on medicine and the support of others, doctors' opinions and hospital personnel, God in the midst of life's cyclones and superficial paradoxes, to survive.

The good news is that Jesus valued that simple trust and faith. He scolds not the children who gather around him, but the disciples, who believe that Jesus is too important and busy to minister to a child. There was purity and unfettered belief in Him, a magnetic pull of love so strong, those children couldn't help themselves. They were drawn to him.

When we are tempted to be disheartened by our inextricable dependence on the support of family, institutions, medications, and doctors, let us remember that Jesus valued child-like faith and dependence on His heavenly Father. In fact, he tells us that those who don't have it won't enter the Kingdom of Heaven. So when was the last time you felt way-too-dependent on something or someone, wishing you had your life more "together," whatever that is.

God wants us to be way-too-dependent on Him. Just how child-like are you?

NOTES

"Everything is possible for him who believes." Mark 9:23b NIV

BELIEF IS THE KEY

Somewhere between the symptoms and the diagnosis, you begin to realize that you're different, not the same as others. Whether it's the mania that leads you to max-out your credit cards, the voices you hear in your head that you know are not your own, or the depression that aches so bad and drains you, you feel suicidal, and uncomfortable with self. You begin to sense the labeling from others, the stigma of the mental illness stereotype. All of this leads you to feel locked into a life that takes you on a bad rollercoaster ride of frightening highs and chilling lows. You feel as if you're always taking three steps forward and two steps back.

You really begin to believe your potential has plummeted, to question if you'll ever get out of the bipolar cycle or if anyone will ever REALLY understand you, and to doubt if you'll ever fulfill your dreams. It hurts.

But Jesus, in this one story of healing a boy with an evil spirit, tells us that belief is the key. Jesus' disciples couldn't heal the boy, so his father begins to falter in his faith that Jesus can heal him. When the father hears Jesus reassure him that he can heal the boy, the father cries out, "I do believe; help me overcome my unbelief!" (Mark 9:24 *NIV)*

When we falter in our faith that God loves us and has good plans for us, we need to cry out to God just as the father did, asking for help believing.

"'I know the plans I have for you,' says the Lord. 'Plans to prosper you and not to harm you, plans to give you a hope and a future.'" Jeremiah 29:11 *NIV.* Believe the Lord is at work in your life to bring about good. Believe in yourself.

NOTES

"Set me free from my prison, that I may praise your name."
Psalm 142:7a NIV

THE DELIVERER

A prison in your mind is far worse than any cell. Born-again inmates often say they had to get locked up to get free on the inside. Jesus Christ is all about freedom, and He has set me free from addictions, institutions, and death. But His greatest deliverance is an inside job.

"For you, O Lord, have delivered my soul from death, my eyes from tears, my feet from stumbling, that I may walk before the Lord in the land of the living." Psalm 116:8-9 *NIV.*

Long months I spent "locked-up" in my mind, playing the same old tapes of anger, resentment, despair, and negative thoughts. My depression was so severe that I spent days isolated in my room all day in the group home, coming out only to smoke and eat. The bars of my prison were reinforced solid steel, made almost escape-proof from years of buying Satan's lies.

"Some sat in darkness and the deepest gloom, prisoners suffering in iron chains, for they had rebelled against the words of God and despised the counsel of the Most High. So he subjected them to bitter labor; they stumbled and there was no one to help. Then they cried to the Lord in their trouble, and he saved them from their distress. He brought them out of the darkness and the deepest gloom and broke away their chains." Psalm 107:10-14 *NIV.*

"If the Son sets you free, you shall be free indeed." In the Gospel John, Jesus declared Himself the Deliverer. No prison cell is too fortified, no addiction is too controlling, and no illness is too overwhelming. He holds the very keys of Hell and death in his hands.

The question is: Do you really want to be free?

If you do, you can begin by thanking and praising God for the good things in your life. Thank Him for the things your chains have taught you. Thank Him that He can set you free.

It may not happen overnight, but deliverance is on the way. . .

NOTES

"Search me, O God, and know my heart, test me and know my anxious thoughts. See if there is any offensive way in me and lead me in the way everlasting." Psalm 139:23-24 NIV.

Meditation versus Self-Medication

Dual diagnosis for those of us with mental illness is high. For some of us, we're not sure which came first: the chicken--mental illness, or the egg--self-medication.

I believe self-medication is anything done to excess (drinking, binge eating, surfing the Internet, chat rooms, gambling, gaming) that ultimately deadens our senses, numbing us to life's hurts, and walling ourselves off from God's light.

My self-medication began at the tender age of 12 when I began reading for hours, isolating and insulating myself in a world I escaped to. I progressed to alcohol at age 15, cigarettes at age 16, marijuana and food at age 17, and obsessive exercising and control eating at age 18. Obsessive running and weight lifting carried me through my twenties, and at age 30, I began to drink alcoholically, which almost prevented me from reaching my forties. I've self-medicated with movies, prescriptions, sugar, caffeine, and shopping, some of which I continue to struggle with.

All this personal research into self-medication has taught me that meditation is a much better way to go.

God Himself tells us in Joshua and Deuteronomy to meditate on His law day and night, filling our minds with words that convict, comfort, heal, strengthen, and encourage us. After living in group homes for over a year and getting nowhere, I began to read God's Word voraciously . . . and something began to happen.

Not in a day, not overnight, but gradually, a transformation took place in my mind. Meditating on God's Word is like sending our brains through a car wash—it gets the dirt and grime out. And it's much less painful and costly than the consequences of self-medication.

The Word says that we are to "take captive every thought to the obedience of Christ."

So let me ask you: Are you the one taking your thoughts captive by meditating on God's Word, or are you Satan's captive, entertaining his thoughts?

NOTES

"Your wound is as deep as the sea. Who can heal you?"
Lamentations 2:13c NIV

"But he was pierced for our transgressions, he was crushed
for our iniquities; the punishment that brought us peace
was upon him, and by his wounds we are healed." Isaiah
53:5 NIV

The Great Physician

All of us at one point in time have been deeply wounded by someone or something. Medically-speaking, a deep wound presents painful problems. If it is not thoroughly-cleaned and bandaged, infection can set in and lead to more serious complications, such as blood poisoning or ultimately amputation.

Physical wounds are similar to spiritual wounds. Many of us with addictions and/or mental illness have been walking around wounded for a long time, and resentment/anger is the infection that has set-in. The wound wasn't ever cleansed by the Holy Spirit, and now we are facing something much more drastic and painful.

As a recovering addict and alcoholic who also happens to be bipolar, I now recognize that I allowed my wounds of the past to become putrid. The infection of resentment poisoned my mind, and the Holy Spirit couldn't heal and cleanse me until I was willing to forgive others. Just as Christ's willing sacrifice was necessary for our forgiveness, our willingness to forgive others is necessary for our own healing.

When I am tempted to hold a grudge or become resentful, I recall these verses from the Sermon on the Mount:

"If you forgive men when they sin against you, your heavenly Father will also forgive you. But if you do not forgive men their sins, your Father will not forgive your sins." (Matt. 6:14-15 *NIV*).

God wants to be your Jehovah Rapha, your Healer, and your Great Physician. He wants you to let go of the wounds of the past and give them to Him. Allow the Holy Spirit to begin the cleansing process by confessing the resentments and anger you've carried. They are the poison we drink to kill someone else.

Ask the Lord to begin working forgiveness and healing in you, even if you don't really want to let it go.

NOTES

"The Spirit of the Sovereign Lord is on me, because the Lord has anointed me to preach good news to the poor. He has sent me to bind up the broken hearted, to proclaim freedom for the captives. . . to bestow on them a crown of beauty instead of ashes, the oil of gladness instead of mourning, and a garment of praise instead of a spirit of despair." Isaiah 61:1-3 NIV

A Crown of Beauty

Have you ever met someone who exudes inner beauty, no matter what they look like? One whose spirit is pure and radiant? They seem to glow with God's goodness.

That is the crown our heavenly Father wants us to wear. Not the ashes of mourning and depression, the gloom and doom of despair. In this passage, Isaiah is bringing wonderful tidings to Israel, foretelling the "good news": Christ the Messiah is coming, Israel's Redeemer! He will bind-up (heal) the brokenhearted; he will set the captives free from sin's oppression.

It's telling that in this passage, Isaiah proclaims the Messiah is coming for the down-and-out: the poor, the brokenhearted, the slaves, the mourning, and those in despair. When Jesus does arrive hundreds of years later, he proclaims that those who aren't sick don't need a physician; he has come for the mentally, physically, emotionally, and spiritually ill.

Christ died for our sins so we can wear our crown of beauty, exude the oil of gladness, and don clothing the gives God rightful praise. As recovering addicts/alcoholics and those living with mental illness, our "stories," or testimonies, have great potential for bringing glory and praise to God, who is our Deliverer.

Thank God today for being your Deliverer, and ask yourself: Is my crown on straight? Do I exude joy or sorrow? Am I wearing—proclaiming—God's praise?

We are living testimonies, and people around us are watching us to see if we look and act like royalty. Let's honor Him today by checking our crown.

NOTES

"Teach me your way, O Lord, and I will walk in your truth; give me an undivided heart, that I may fear your name.. . For great is your love toward me; you have delivered me from the depths of the grave." Psalm 86:11, 13 NIV

A Divided Heart

"A house divided will soon fall," said Jesus. So it is with our hearts if they are divided---not our physical heart that pumps our blood, but what we cherish and desire, the things we spend our time and money on. These are the things that steer the course of our life, either charting us through deep waters, navigating through storms, or bashing us upon the rocks and reefs, shipwrecking us.

Through most of my life, my heart was divided between things of the flesh I desired—food, alcohol, affection, drugs, clothes, approval of peers, social acceptance, money to shop, fine furniture to fill my house, maxing out credit cards—and the spiritual things of God I knew I should desire.

The result of this divided heart was a double life, one in which I truly believed I could keep one foot in the world and one foot pursuing God, straddling the fence. It didn't work.

"Every kingdom divided against itself will be ruined, and every city or household divided against itself will not stand." (Matt. 12:25b *NIV*) A divided heart leads to the depths of the grave, a dark place of no peace and no rest, where Satan's dominion defeats and destroys.

But an undivided heart fears God's name. This is a fear of reverence and respect for the One who rescues and redeems us from the grave. It is a heart that longs for righteousness, truth, obedience to God's Word, and wholeness.

Where is your heart steering the course of your life? Are you shipwrecked and sending out an SOS? God wants all of you---your heart, soul, strength, and mind. Give him all of your heart today.

NOTES

"Why do you look at the speck of sawdust in your brother's eye and pay no attention to the plank in your own eye? How can you say to your brother, 'Let me take the speck out of your eye,' when all the time there is a plank in your own eye? You hypocrite, first take the plank out of your own eye, and then you will see clearly to remove the speck from your brother's eye." Matthew 7:3-5 NIV

SPECK-BUSTERS

In recovery from addictions and mental illness, many people along your path will offer well-meaning advice. Some will speak with the voice of experience; others, while they may have your best interest at heart, will just tell you what you should do. Their expectation is that you will follow their advice and your life will instantly improve. These are the people you want to avoid-—I call them "speck-busters".

"Speck-busters" are always on the lookout for flaws in others. They abrasively and hastily tell you what's wrong with your life, while remaining oblivious to their own flaws. Their "quick-fix" solutions to your character defects lack the wisdom, insight, and genuine concern for your recovery. Their focus on your speck instead of their log really undermines their credibility, making them bothersome busy-bodies and hypocrites at best.

Neither recovery from addictions nor mental illness has a quick-fix as a cure. In fact, the term "cure" is not relevant with either—there is no cure from alcoholism, crack addiction, bipolar disorder, or schizophrenia. What is relevant is a course of recovery, a plan flexible enough to roll with the punches life serves up . . . to help you move forward when you've just taken two steps back.

Jesus, in the Beatitudes, tells us that we must examine our own lives for character defects before we begin to try to take inventory for others. "Speck-busters" also turn out to be "hope-busters," which recovering addicts and those struggling with recovery from mental illness don't need. Life and recovery are processes, journeys of trial and error, successes and set-backs.

We don't need speck-busters.

"God opposes the proud but gives grace to the humble."
Proverbs 3:34

"Humble yourselves before the Lord and he will lift you up."
James 4:10NIV

HUMILITY

Practicing humility is both a discipline and a state of mind. Paul, in Il Corinthians 12:7-10 *NIV,* states, "To keep me from becoming conceited . . . there was given me a thorn in my flesh, a messenger of Satan, to torment me. Three times I pled with the Lord to take it away from me. But he said to me, 'My grace is sufficient for you, for my power is made perfect in weakness.' Therefore, I will boast all the more gladly about my weaknesses, so that Christ's power may rest on me. . . For when I am weak, then I am strong."

In my weakened state of addiction and mental illness, I cried out to God over and over again to "deliver" me, asking "Why me?!" It never even crossed my mind that His power would be showcased if mine was gone. Powerlessness is what we addicts and alcoholics admit to first. We no longer have the personal pride and power to say "no". We must depend on Christ's power to make us strong. We must practice dependence on God to stay alive.

I try to no longer ask God why I was given the "thorns" of mental illness and addictions. A trip to the Emergency Room, which almost led to a week's stay in the psychiatric ward, answered all my lingering doubts. It had been almost five years since I had been hospitalized, a fact that I was somewhat proud of.

But it took only A WEEK of severe depression, isolating, and self-medicating to almost land me right back in a place I loathe to go—all because I'm powerless, and my recovery today depends on how powerful my God is. We must humble ourselves daily to get the go-juice of the grace we need and the power of the Holy Spirit to live it out.

When was the last time you got on your knees and bowed before Him?

NOTES

"Fear not, for I have redeemed you. I have summoned you by name; you are mine. When you pass through the waters, I will be with you; and when you pass through the rivers, they will not sweep over you. When you walk through the fire, you will not be burned; the flames will not set you ablaze. For I am the Lord your God, the Holy One of Israel, your Savior. . ." Isaiah 43:1 b-3a NIV

THROUGH THE FIRE

After I received my DUI, my mother broke it to me that she and my father had decided it was best if I lived in a group home. They didn't have guardianship of me, so I could have bucked it. But I decided to honor them as my parents, and I needed a safe place where getting alcohol would have been nearly impossible.

Mind-numbing, stir-crazy days of sitting in the smoke room, laying in my bed, dreading each new day as being more depressing than the last, being fed prison-quality food, sharing a bathroom with two men and two women, who frequently left 'surprises' for the next occupant, sharing a room with a woman who liked the thermostat on 80 degrees both summer and winter, living with residents who frequently soiled their pants, bummed cigarettes, and had no table manners left me almost completely despondent. I was utterly without hope; I gave up living life.

God, however, never gave up on me. As a child of God, He had "summoned me by name." As dreadful and difficult as those eight months was, I can look back on it now as the means and motivation for staying dry during an early, critical juncture in my sobriety.

We have all placed ourselves in positions where someone else was calling the shots because we couldn't handle the responsibilities of living. While in such a position, we may feel demeaned and demoralized, yet the humble realization that we couldn't make it on our own should produce in us a thankfulness that God picked up the broken pieces while we were shattered. He kept the rivers from sweeping us away. He kept the furnace from setting us ablaze.

Thank God today for redeeming your life from the pit. It's hard to be thankful for that until you've experienced what the pit is.

NOTES

"Make it your ambition to lead a quiet life, to mind your own business and to work with your hands, just as we told you, so that your daily life may win the respect of outsiders and so that you will not be dependent on anybody." 1 Thessalonians 4:11-12 NIV

"Whatever you do, work at it with all your heart, as working for the Lord, not for men, since you know that you will receive an inheritance from the Lord as a reward. It is the Lord Christ you are serving." Colossians 3:23-24 NIV

BUSY HANDS

Where there is addiction and/or mental illness, idle hands are the devil's work shop. Too much "down time" leads to rumination, and often, stinking thinking, which traps us in the past. Group homes, which are largely holding tanks for the chemically and mentally-challenged, are often literal wastelands of untapped human potential. Little or nothing is provided to engage clients in hobbies, crafts, handiwork, or other mentally-stimulating activities that involve the hands as well as the head.

There are as many creative outlets we can plug into as our imagination and talents allow, but here are a few I've found therapeutic in the last decade:

1) Artwork — I took a basic art course in college, and a calligraphy class at a local community college. I began making "Scripture Pictures", Bible verses done in calligraphy arranged with dried flowers and plants, and framed them. I bought old frames from second-hand stores and painted them, often using sponging techniques to give them an antiqued-finish. I then sold them or gave them as gifts. I even had a booth at a flea market and sold them.

   I have served as an informal art instructor for my niece and nephews, who are homeschooled. Pastels are my favorite to work with, although they are somewhat pricey. Framing the artwork preserves it and adds importance to it.

2) Gardening and canning — If you're physically able, this is one of the most satisfying hobbies to have, with the bonuses of physical exertion and being able to enjoy the fruits of your labor. Making all kinds of pickles, salsas, and homemade preserves was always well-worth the effort. Canned items make excellent gifts as well.

3) Writing — From writing for a Christian monthly to personal journal writing, this is by far the most therapeutic "work" I've enjoyed. It's an outlet for my thoughts and feelings, helping me "resolve" issues.

Find your creative outlets and get plugged in!

"He was despised and rejected by men, a man of sorrows, and familiar with grief. Like one from whom men hide their faces; he was despised and we esteemed him not" Isaiah 53:3 NIV

HIDDEN FACES

Mental illness and addictions are tragedies others prefer not to confront in daily life. When the businessman crosses the street so he won't have to deal with the wino on the sidewalk, talking out of his head, he's "hiding his face." People often feel uncomfortable dealing with people who have mental illness or addictions because they present "unknowns" into life's equation, and this makes many of them uneasy.

Then, there are the stigmas attached to both mental illness and addiction: slow, stupid, crazy, deranged, weak-willed, lazy, delusional, dangerous, worthless. It's an uphill battle confronting these labels head on in the workplace, social arena, and family relations, and it can leave one feeling much the way Christ was described in the prophecy in Isaiah 53:3 *NIV:*

1) Despised- Jesus told the truth, and many men hated Him for it. They believed he was just a carpenter from Nazareth.

2) Rejected- Christ was mocked, insulted, asked to leave towns, and rejected by many who found his teaching too difficult.

3) Man of Sorrows- He carried the weight of the sin debt of the world to His cross.

4) Familiar with suffering-After healing all kinds of diseases and illness, He was well-acquainted with the sufferer's grief. He suffered much at the cross.

5) He was not esteemed- God Incarnate comes to earth, and people reject Him because He challenged their faith. He says things that make them very uncomfortable, and He comes as a poor carpenter from Nazareth.

Jesus identifies with you in these feelings, for He experienced them, too. Take solace with Him and keep pushing forward!

"You have been a refuge for the poor, a refuge for the needy in his distress, a shelter from the storm, and a shade from the heat. . The sovereign Lord will wipe away the tears from all faces; he will remove the disgrace of his people from all the earth. The Lord has spoken." Isaiah 25:4-8 NIV

No More Tears

The polar opposites of mania (highs) and depression (lows) are the equivalent of a nightmarish emotional roller coaster ride that leaves you begging to get off. I remember being admitted to one psychiatric ward after a terrible two-week episode of manic paranoia and suicidal depression. I paced the hallway of the ward for three to four hours, unable to stop crying. It wasn't a muffled whimper or silent tears, but a wailing, a mourning of the death of a part of me.

Each of us experiences mourning in our lifetimes, periods of loss so tragic that we can't do anything but cry. Some of us have bottled-up hurt and other emotions for so long, we are like a dam that breaks, bursting forth the full force of feelings in the release of crying.

This passage assures us that the Lord is close to the brokenhearted, providing peace in a time of storm, shelter for the downcast and heavy-laden.

Many feel disgraced when they cry publicly, but this passage reassures us that God will remove humiliation from His people. Think about all the things you have been disgraced by- the stigma of addiction/mental illness, the humiliation of loss of loved ones, jobs, social status, and perceived mental capacity- all devastating blows to your identity. The Lord will one day remove all that disgrace from the earth. It will be wiped away, just as our tears.

"*The son said to him, 'Father, I have sinned against heaven and against you. I am no longer worthy to be called your son.' But the father said to his servants, 'Quick! Bring the best robe and put it on him. Put a ring on his finger and sandals on his feet. Bring the fattened calf and kill it. Let's have a feast and celebrate. For this son of mine was dead and is alive again; . . .'" Luke 15: 21-22 NIV*

CELEBRATE SURVIVAL

I challenge you to look back at the last 25 years of your life, and survey the damage: the lost dreams, jobs, and relationships; the time squandered living in a bottle or crack pipe; the lost freedoms in group homes, hospitals, institutions, and prisons; the countless hours in rehabs, courts, jails, and guardianships.

Now, look at the flipside- you survived! Not only should we celebrate survival each day, but we should celebrate the new life we have in Jesus, who gives it abundantly.

The story of the prodigal son is quite fitting for those recovering from alcohol, drugs or mental illness. The son takes his portion of the inheritance and goes far away, squandering the money on wine, women and song. When the money is gone, his "fast friends" disappear and a tragic famine strikes. He is forced to do the most despicable work a Jew could do- tending pigs. He was so hungry, he longed to eat the pods fed to the pigs! He comes to his senses, realizing he can return home as a servant. But his father, who runs to greet him will hear nothing of it- he throws a banquet for his return.

God is the father, waiting to throw the banquet and we are the prodigal son. Have you returned home to celebrate?

"The Lord God took the man and put him in the Garden of Eden to work it and take care of it. And the Lord God commanded the man, 'You are free to eat from any tree in the garden; but you must not eat from the tree of the knowledge of good and evil, when you eat of it, you will surely die.'"
Genesis 2:15-17 NIV

Setting Boundaries

God was the first boundary-setter. He instructed Adam and Eve that they could eat from any tree in the garden except the tree of knowledge of good and evil. Their breaking of the boundary that God set for their good has had immeasurable and devastating consequences to mankind ever since. The Mosaic Law (including the 10 Commandments) was the sum of God's boundaries given to the Israelites in the Old Testament.

Boundaries are restrictions or limits enforced in relationships for the welfare of both parties. Anytime we violate God's law, we are breaking a boundary- sinning.

As recovering addicts, alcoholics and those living with mental illness, we have problems with boundaries- knowing our limits, resisting the urge to manipulate and be manipulated, being co-dependent, knowing when to say "yes" and when to say a resounding "no!" and understanding where we end and others begin.

Because some of our relationships are so toxic, we must guard our boundaries wisely. For some of us, this means restricting or breaking off the relationship with another. It may mean setting up clear parameters that are not to be trespassed. We must guard our boundaries closely for allowing them to be violated leads us to jails, institutions and death. We must honor God's boundaries or laws because they are for our own well-being.

"Now Abel kept flocks, and Cain worked the soil. In the course of time, Cain brought some of the fruits of the soil as an offering to the Lord. But Abel brought fat portions from some of the first born of his flock. The Lord looked with favor on Abel and his offering, but on Cain and his offering he did not look with favor. So Cain was very angry, and his face was downcast." Genesis 26:5 NIV

DYSFUNCTION JUNCTION

After the fall of man, when sin and its consequences permeated all aspects of life on earth, we are introduced to the first dysfunctional family: Adam and Eve, and their sons, Cain and Abel. Cain was so enraged that the Lord was pleased with his younger brother's sacrifice, Cain led him to a field and murdered him.

Every family on earth has some dysfunction, but it seems those of us in recovery had more dysfunction than others. Some of us had parents who were addicts or alcoholics, while others of us suffered mental, emotional, spiritual, and physical scaring and abuse that we've carried all of our lives.

It's time to blow through Dysfunction Junction, and ride the Grace Train to the next stop, Transformation Station, where as Romans 12:1-2 *NIV* says, we are to be "transformed by the renewing of our mind." This is the end of the line, folks. If we aren't reading God's Word daily to allow the Holy Spirit to work in our hearts and minds, our minds will stay in that funky dysfunction- stinking thinking. As believers, we have at our disposal the mind of Christ, but we must pray for it and cultivate it by becoming intimately acquainted with Him. The miracle of true transformation happens first in the heart, soul and mind. Outward transformation is last!

"For I was hungry and you gave me something to eat, I was thirsty and you gave me something to drink, I was a stranger and you invited me in, I needed clothes and you clothed me, I was sick and you looked after me, I was in prison and you came to visit me." Matthew 25:35-36 NIV

THE LEAST OF THESE

The general population doesn't think too highly of those with addictions and/or mental illness. The social stigmas, avoidance, and roadblocks all put those recovering in the category of "the least of these," as Jesus called them- the individuals in society that are seen as least important. Thank heavens Jesus didn't think so.

In fact, Jesus went out of his way to minister healing and hope to the down and out. He had the disciples row all the way to an island to heal one man who was so mentally ill and demon possessed that no one could keep him bound in chains. The Bible says that after Jesus cast the legions of demons out of him, he was clothed and in his right mind.

Jesus healed lepers and never worried about associating with outcasts in Jewish society. He allowed a prostitute to wash his feet with her hair and tears. He told the disciples not to hinder the children from coming to Him, and He rubbed elbows so closely with common men that a sick woman who was ceremonially "unclean" was healed by touching Him. Shouldn't we value the least, too?

"For you have spent enough time in the past doing what the pagans choose living in debauchery, lust, drunkenness, orgies, carousing and detestable idolatry". I Peter 4:3 NIV

How Much is Enough?

When we survey the wreckage of our past, one thing is clear: we wasted too much time. All the time we spent in the bottom of a bottle, at the end of a needle, strung out or looking for a fix, in a jail cell or a hospital bed, consulting the committee in our heads, in our own world thinking it revolved around us, paranoid about everyone doing us in, resentful because people didn't meet our expectations, cold and indifferent because we didn't want anyone to know we cared.

As the Holy Spirit transforms us to glorify God, we recognize that in our addictions and illnesses, we wasted the precious hours, days, weeks and years of our lives. The good news is that the Lord can take that senseless waste and use it to glorify Himself. He can "restore the years that the locust has eaten," and give us the most productive life for His kingdom.

Peter says in these verses, "Enough! You've spent too much time living like those without God do."Promise yourself today that you're going to "redeem the time," making the most of every God-given opportunity. Share your hope with someone who needs it. Live today as though it was your last day on earth. Ask God to bring opportunities to help others your way. Ask Jesus to help you be more like Him. Close the door on the wreckage of your past and move into the here-and-now that the Lord has for you. That knock on your door, phone ringing or helping hand you give is your chance.

NOTES

"See I have refined you, though not as silver: I have tried and chosen you in the furnace of affliction. For my own sake, for my own sake, I do it. How can I let myself be defamed? I will not yield my glory to another." Isaiah 48:10-11 NIV

THE FURNACE OF AFFLICTION- PART ONE

The summer of 2007 was the worst train wreck of my mental illness I had experienced thus far. I woke up one Saturday morning that February before and was certain I was going to kill myself with drinking if I didn't stop. I started walking for one hour early in the morning, attending AA meetings, and began drinking only Crystal Lite. These were all positive steps, but I left one necessary step out: I didn't start taking my Lithium. By the beginning of May, I was in full manic mode, only sleeping 3 to 4 hours a night, stressed out about teaching, and growing paranoid. My mom recognized something was wrong and took me to a large treatment center with a psychiatric unit. I didn't go peacefully. I had to be held-down and given a shot. For 6 to 8 hours, I was confined to the psych's holding tank, a large room with only beds and bathrooms. The windows were covered with metal screens to prevent anyone from breaking them.

Once I got out in the ward's "regular" population, other problems arose. I was so overmedicated, I was unable to shower by myself, or do any other personal hygiene; I cried at the drop of a hat, often because I thought people were laughing at me; and we had a mini staff-client riot when some patients felt they were being treated unfairly and started throwing fruit at the staff. I slipped in and out of reality, delusional at times, and it seemed that month would never be over.

One Saturday during visitation, my sister snuck a Bible into me with many Scriptures underlined to encourage me. She cried when she saw me because I looked so bad. I felt I was slowly understanding what the "furnace of affliction" meant. It was only the beginning.

NOTES

"Before I was afflicted I went astray, but now I obey your word." Psalm 119: 67 NIV

"It was good for me to be afflicted so that I might learn your decrees." Psalm 119: 71 NIV

THE FURNACE OF
AFFLICTION- PART TWO

Only a week out of the first hospital, I entered a second one in a different state. I was still manic and delusional. The psych unit at this facility was tiny, and I remember pacing up and down the hallway feeling like a rat in a maze.

There was a panoramic picture window that overlooked a lovely park with a pond and ducks, children playing while parents looked on, owners walking their dogs, and people generally enjoying and getting on with their lives. It seemed I was frozen in time, stuck with my illness. I was a prisoner in my own mind.

"Therefore, I urge you brothers, in view of God's mercy, to offer your bodies as living sacrifices, holy and pleasing to God- this is your spiritual act of worship. Do not conform any longer to the pattern of this world, but be transformed by the renewing of your mind. Then you will be able to test and approve what God's will is- His good, pleasing and perfect will." Romans 12:1-2 *NIV.* This process of transformation that Romans speaks to is not a one-time, done deal. It is a daily offering of yourself to pursue holiness by reading and meditating on God's Word, praying and seeking the kingdom of God here and now. The dross of our lives that God wants to burn off in the furnace of affliction is anything that smacks of the world and competes with Him for our attention. His Word literally changes our minds, freeing us to obey Him rather than be held hostage by the world and Satan's lies. God uses our afflictions of addictions and mental illness to draw us closer to Him- to learn His laws so that we might be set free.

NOTES

"I know, Lord, that your laws are righteous, and in faithfulness you have afflicted me. May your unfailing love be my comfort, according to your promise to your servant." Psalm 119:75-76 NIV

"Though He slay me, yet will I trust Him." Job 13:15 NIV

FURNACE OF AFFLICTION-
PART THREE

After two weeks in the second hospital, I was sent in shackles, in a highway patrol car, to the state mental hospital. I guess the changes to my medications at the second hospital weren't working out so well. The shackles are to keep patients safe, but believe me, you feel like a prisoner going away for a long time. My family wondered if the "old me" would ever re-surface. I felt trapped in a nightmare I couldn't wake up from, and my solace was reading God's Word and praying to Him. At night, I slept with my Bible on my chest, and it comforted me. During the day, I paced the short hallways we had, even though my gait was unsteady from being overmedicated. One of the most difficult aspects of being confined to a psych ward is dealing with other patients. Their paranoia, grandiose thinking, and distorted ideas affected everyone around them. One guy thought our unit was full of FBI and CIA agents. I assured him that I wasn't one. About six times a day we got smoke breaks and got to go outside. Large fences with barbed wire at the top were not-so-subtle reminders that you weren't going anywhere.

Once a week you met with your doctor and other staff in a board room to discuss your case. I remember the doctor telling me that if I ever stopped taking my medicine again and ended up back there, I would probably have to live in a group home setting the rest of my life. I guess he was trying to scare me straight, if that's possible with mental illness. I knew that God had allowed this pain for a reason; I just had no earthly clue at the time why.

NOTES

"*Though the mountains be shaken and the hills be removed, yet my unfailing love for you will not be shaken, nor my covenant of peace be removed, says the Lord who has compassion on you.*" *Isaiah 54:10 NIV*

WHEN THE WORLD IS
UPSIDE DOWN

My mother and stepfather picked me up from the state mental hospital and had agreed to care for me until I felt well enough to live alone again. My mountains had been shaken. I had been in hospitals the entire summer, but God had provided guardian angels to watch over me. His love was not shaken.

I was not "well" when I returned to their home. My gait was so bad from overmedication, I walked with great difficulty. My mother frequently had to hold my hand. Being out in public, listening to loud movies and the television were so over stimulating to me. I had to get away. My thinking was still distorted- not always based in reality. I still did "strange" things, like going out on the porch in the middle of the night and not turning on the lights or putting on shoes.

One morning I went out on the porch right before dawn. I remember sitting there having a conversation with God, begging and pleading with Him to please send Christ back to the earth to gather the saints, to end the terrible pain and suffering everywhere. I asked Him why He was tarrying- what was taking so long?

I looked up at the horizon, and there in the clouds was the word, "Israel." Now some would say I was hallucinating, but I believe God speaks to and through the mentally ill in special ways.

Our mediator of a better covenant is Jesus Christ, who will return to earth for His bride, the church, when she is complete. We can experience His covenant of peace through salvation now, even when the hills are removed and the mountains shake. He is a compassionate God.

NOTES

"As for God, His way is perfect; the word of the Lord is flawless. He is a shield for all who take refuge in Him . . . It is God who arms me with strength and makes my way perfect. He makes my feet like the feet of a deer; he enables to stand on heights." Psalm 18:30, 32-33 NIV

BALANCING ON LIFE'S TIGHTROPE

As recovering addicts/alcoholics and those dealing a mental disorder, it seems that maintaining balance in our personal lives is much like walking a tightrope without a safety net.

So much a part of our illness is black or white, all-or-nothing thinking. We believe in order to do something right, we must go all-out or full-on, neglecting the other necessary components of life that help steady us.

Maintaining a well-balanced life is key to our success. If I sleep too much, I am lethargic and isolated. If I spend too much of my paycheck on gifts for others, I don't have enough to pay bills and buy groceries. If I spend all my time reading the Bible or attending meetings, I won't be able to put into practice with others what I learn.

My tightrope, if I lose my balance, has depression on one side of the rope and mania on the other. I have fallen off both sides countless times, but God's safety net has always caught me. As frightening and difficult as it seems to climb the ladder to get back on again, God has always given me the courage to do so.

David, in Psalm 18, says that it is God who makes our way perfect-- not us. He makes our feet strong and sure-footed like a deer, able to scale mountains and view life from the summits. Ask God today to arm you with the strength to maintain balance in your life so you stand on the heights.

NOTES

"Why are you downcast, O my soul? Why so disturbed within me? Put your hope in God, for I will yet praise him, My Savior and My God." Psalm 42:5-6a NIV

"My tears have been my food day and night . . ." Psalm 42:3a NIV

"I am feeble and utterly crushed; I groan in anguish of heart. All my longings lie open before you, O Lord; My heart pounds, my strength fails me; even the light has gone from my eyes." Psalm 38:8-10 NIV

WINNING THE WAR

"Suicide is Painless," the theme song to the hit series MASH in the 70's, depicts the act of ending one's life as an empowering choice in the face of war. But suicide, no matter how viable an option it seems, is the tragic snuffing out of a magnificent candle that once burned brightly.

The Big Book of Alcoholics Anonymous declares that acceptance is the answer to all my problems today. Let us remember that we are in a war-- a spiritual, mental, physical, and emotional war every day. The war of addiction and/or mental illness becomes so wearisome, so relentless, that we must fight the urge to surrender to the defeating, deafening voices in our head. The battles, individually- identified and prepared for, are the keys to winning the war. We must strategize and determine daily battles to train for such as: 1) activities and interaction with people that boosts our self-esteem and gives us daily purpose; 2) a schedule of daily habits/rituals that order our lives and help us achieve self-maintenance; 3) daily recreation/enrichment activities that help us love, laugh, and unwind; and 4) a daily regiment of time spent praying and reading God's Word.

Countless times, my perceived reality was so unbearably miserable, I had thoughts of ending it. In fact, one chilly December morning, with house slippers on and no coat, I walked all the way from my apartment to the Mississippi River to jump in. Thank heavens onlookers prevented me from following through. That was one of my harrowing escapes from death. We must put our hope in Him to win the war.

"In the year that King Uzziah died, I saw the Lord seated on a throne, high and exalted and the train of his robe filled the temple. Above him were seraphs, each with six wings. With two wings they covered their faces, with two wings they covered their feet, and with two they were flying. And they were calling to one another: holy, holy, holy is the Lord Almighty; the whole earth is full of His glory." Isaiah 6.1-3 NIV

ENLARGED VISION

Those of us who suffer from mental illness, in our manic phase, somehow believe we can save the world with our suggestions, shoulder superhuman strength and wisdom, and juggle twenty-four tasks simultaneously. The end result is chaotic; the cause is grandiose thinking.

God wants us to have a proper perspective of ourselves and a lofty view of Himself. He is the Shepherd, and we are the sheep (Psalm 23 *NIV*); He is the Creator and sustainer (Psalm 100 *NIV*) and we are the created; He is the Alpha and the Omega (Revelation I :8*NIV*) and we are finite, locked into space and time. We are weak, but He is strong.

Yet, Paul says in Philippians that "I can do all things through Christ who strengthens me." (Phil. 4:13 *NIV*) We, as Christians, have available to us Christ's power to help us do ANYTHING! "Nothing is too difficult for Thee," says David in the Psalms. Paul again says in Romans 8:37 *NIV* that "We are more than conquerors in Christ . ." and God's strength is "made perfect in our weakness." (II Corinthians 12:9 *NIV*)

Let us enlarge our perspective on God: "For my thoughts are not your thoughts, neither are your ways My ways," declares the Lord. "As the heavens are higher than the earth, so are My ways higher than your ways and My thoughts than your thoughts." (Isaiah 55:8-9 *NIV*)

"As a father has compassion on his children, so the Lord has compassion on those who fear Him; for he knows how we are formed, he remembers that we are dust. As for man, his days are like grass . . . the wind blows over it and it is gone . . ." Psalm 103:13-16 *NIV*. Respect your limits and trust a limitless God!

"The Lord will call you back as if you were a wife deserted and distressed in spirit—a wife who married young, only to be rejected," says your God. "For brief moment I abandoned you, but with deep compassion I will bring you back." Isaiah 34:6-7 NIV

REJECTION

It's a painful part of the human experience. For some of us, it happened early on, when a parent emotionally or physically abandoned us, leaving us feeling unloved. For others, the trauma occurred in grade school when peers humiliated and excluded you, flashbacks that seem as real today as they did years ago.

Perhaps your rejection has been in the work arena. No matter how hard you try, you can't seem to hold a job. Others squeeze you out of position and bosses let you go. Job hunting becomes a painful reminder of short stints on your resume.

Or maybe it was a deep and personal rejection by a spouse that sent you reeling. Your mental illness, social stigma, or self-medication was more than they could handle.

No matter how we experience rejection, it scars us, disfiguring a part of our heart. To be "deserted and distressed in spirit" can lead us to places of anguish or bitterness, opening emotional wounds afresh and leading us to self-medicate. But if we are a child of God, we can rebuke Satan's spirit of rejection, filling our minds instead with the truths of who we are according to God's Word: beloved, a chosen people, a priestly nation, heirs of the kingdom of God and co-heirs with Christ, a royal kingdom, seated with Christ in the heavenlies, more than conquerors, a living epistle of the power of God, redeemed by the blood of the Lamb. God's deep compassion for us wants to restore the wound of rejection we experience. Ask Him to help you refuse the spirit of rejection in your life.

"Forget the former things; do not dwell on the past. See, I am doing a new thing! Now it springs up; do you not perceive it? I am making a way in the in the wasteland." Isaiah 43:18-19

Cultivating Hope

"Without hope" described me best my first eight years of bipolar illness. I spent 50-60% of my waking hours reviewing all the "doors" that had closed, never to open again. My stinking thinking and my analysis paralysis left me stuck, never realizing nor believing that God was doing a new thing.

God says in this passage we are not to dwell on the past. I had a list a mile long of all the hurts, frustrations, resentments, and regrets I reviewed daily that kept me from living in the magnificent present. Maybe your present isn't so magnificent, and you're desperately longing for the good 'ole days, convinced no one can reach you in your addiction/mental illness now and give you hope.

You've been stranded in the Sahara Desert of addiction/mental illness, convinced there's no way out with no helicopter to rescue you, no camel with humps large enough to carry you through. The temptation to give up is overwhelming because your canteen is dry. Suddenly, God bursts into the situation with an all-terrain vehicle, an unlimited amount of gas and an oasis right where it is needed, where He provides sustenance for our trip. God always makes a way for us in life's deserts, and He brings delicacies for us to delight in.

Walk away from those closed doors of the past and look expectantly for God to open doors for the present that lead to the future. He is the Hope giver. He wants to make a way in your desert.

"Love covers a multitude of sins." I Peter 4:8 NIV

"Bear with each other and forgive whatever grievances you may have against one another. Forgive as the Lord forgave you." Colossians 2:13 NIV

BEARING WITH ONE ANOTHER

A reoccurring lesson that God continues to teach me, but I resist, is forgiveness. While some people allow others' mean-spirited comments and rude/hurtful actions to roll right off their backs, not phased by the injury or insult, I believe I must be the most sensitive human on the planet, ready to cry, retaliate, or whimper at the drop of a hat! It seems that I am so easily irritated, hurt, or angered by those in close proximity to me, my natural defense is to isolate, walling myself off from the offenders. Of course, this is not the course of action Jesus instructs.

"For if you forgive men when they sin against you, your heavenly Father will also forgive you. But if you do not forgive men their sins, your Father will not forgive your sins." Matthew 6:14-15 *NIV*

Those of us coping with a mental illness have both a heap of forgiving to offer others and ask others for. Let go of the anger that binds you by starting with forgiveness. Love goes a lot further than a grievance.

"Hope deferred makes the heart sick, but a longing fulfilled is a tree of life." Proverbs 13:12 NIV

HUMAN HOPE IS FRAGILE: DREAMS FULFILLED BY GOD ARE FORTIFYING

Most of us in recovery have had years of heart sickness from hopes deferred. Perhaps those deferred dreams and hopes were why we picked up the bottle or pipe in the first place, or we found ourselves so heart-sick from loss, pain, or abuse that we crossed over that thin line of mental health into illness.

Our hopes and dreams are like a butterfly—fragile, elusive, and beautiful-- just out-of- reach at times, and at others, right in front of us, so tangible we can touch them. David in the Psalms tells us: "Delight yourself in the Lord and He will give you the desires of your heart." Psalm 37:4 *NIV*

God the Father knows each of us so intimately. He knows our deep desires, hopes and dreams. Better yet, He wants to fulfill them, but there is a condition: we must find our joy and delight in Him first and foremost. He wants first place in our hearts, souls, strength, and minds. Our Father wants our hope to be a solid trust in the work of Jesus Christ: "We have this hope as an anchor for the soul, firm and secure. It enters the inner sanctuary behind the curtain where Jesus, who went before us, has entered on our behalf." Hebrews 6:19-20a *NIV.* Jesus is our Tree of Life! He longs to fulfill every good purpose He has for us.

"But you are a chosen people, a royal priesthood, a holy nation, a people belonging to God, that you might declare the praises of Him who called you out of darkness into His wonderful light. Once you were not a people, but now you are the people of God; once you had not received mercy, but now you have received mercy." I Peter 2:9-10 NIV

LIVING OUT YOUR TRUE IDENTITY

Imagine waking up one morning and discovering you were a relative of royalty. You quickly dressed, were whisked away to the airport to catch a private jet, and then chauffeured to the royal palace in a limousine, where you met your new relatives. Sounds like a fairy tale?

However, the minute we become God's children by accepting Christ as our Savior, amazing things happen! The Bible says that all of heaven rejoices when one person enters the kingdom. Your name is written in the Lamb's Book of Life. You are transferred from the domain of darkness into the family of the King, the kingdom of light.

"As you come to Him, the living stone—rejected by men but chosen by God and precious to Him—you also, like living stones, are being built into a spiritual house to be a royal priesthood, offering spiritual sacrifices acceptable to God through Jesus Christ." I Peter 2:4-5 *NIV.* In the old covenant, only the priests could offer sacrifices and atone for the people's sins. In the new covenant that Jesus Christ inaugurated for us by His death on the cross, He is our High Priest who forever lives to intercede on our behalf. We have access to His Throne 24-7 because we are a child of the King. May our lives be spiritual sacrifices pleasing to Him and always honoring the King.

"For He will deliver the needy who cry out, the afflicted who have no one to help. He will take pity on the weak and the needy and save the needy from death." Psalm 72: 12-13 NIV

"You are my hiding place; you will protect me from trouble and surround me with songs of deliverance." Psalm 32: 7 NIV

HIDING PLACE

As children, most of us had a "secret" hiding place, a place we could find comfort and solitude in when our little worlds weren't quite what we wanted them to be. In the closet, under the stairs, in our tree house, or our bedroom closet, we retreated when the outside world seemed cruel, perplexing, or unfair.

In Psalm 32, David tells the Lord that He is his hiding place. David needed strong hiding places—King Saul was jealously determined to kill David, and forced David to live like a vagabond, in and out of caves for years while he and his army hunted him.

In our metamorphosis from addiction and mental illness, we need a hiding place where we can retreat from our chaotic worlds, be protected from the voices in our heads, telling us all the things we don't need to dwell on, and be surrounded instead by the Lord's songs of deliverance. The Lord wants to be YOUR hiding place, where you run for strength to face giants, cry out in confession of your sin, and plead for mercy and deliverance.

"No temptation has seized you except what is common to man. And God is faithful. He will not let you be tempted beyond what you can bear. But when you are tempted, He will also provide a way out so that you can stand up under it." I Corinthians 10: 13 NIV

SETTING BOUNDARIES FOR SANITY AND SOBRIETY

Why is it that those we love the most usually hurt us the most? Of course, our honesty, transparency, and intimacy with them open the door to our heart, allowing pain, disillusionment and judgmentalism to creep in. Relationships in which there has been verbal, physical, or emotional abuse present sticky issues for boundary-setting, but it must be done, especially if these people are controllers.

Detaching ourselves from toxic controllers, inside or outside of our families, allows us to hear the Holy Spirit in our lives. If we're too busy trying to please or placate the controllers, we're in the problem, not the solution. God is a jealous God who wants our undivided attention. He wants our sole focus to be pleasing Him!

When I have run-ins with toxic controllers, I can get stuck in stinking thinking, based solely on what this person had said to 'control' me, demeaning and depressing me! But the Lord is faithful! I usually don't give in to those despondent thoughts for long. The Holy Spirit prompts me that I need to detoxify my life and not be tempted to give in to despair.

"See to it that no one falls short of the grace of God and that no root of bitterness springs up, causing trouble and by it, defiling many." Hebrews 12:15 NIV

Get to the Root of It

As recovering alcoholics and addicts and those dealing with mental illness, our relationships are often wrought with tension, hurtful words, and calloused indifference.

My natural, knee-jerk response to these relationship interactions is deep-seeded anger and the temptation to ruminate on it, thus becoming bitter, which ultimately lead to despair and despondency. But I somehow have to muddle through those dark emotions to get to the root of the bitterness and let it go. How is that done? Only with the power of the Holy Spirit, shedding of tears, and a life-changing view of myself as seen through the eyes or the Father due to the blood of Jesus Christ.

My bitterness springs from a root of rejection at a young age. I'm overly sensitive to criticism, I have poor self-esteem, I have perfectionist tendencies to mask my inadequacies, I'm obsessive-compulsive, I have a tendency to seek approval/people please, and have dark mood swings on roller coasters of emotion. But my heavenly Father sees me spotless—unblemished. "Come, now, let us reason together," says the Lord. "Though your sins are like scarlet, they shall be as white as snow; though they are red as crimson, they shall be like wool." Isaiah 1: 18 *NIV*

Christ came to purchase us with His precious blood and in that alone we know we are loved by Him! He sees us as beautiful, no matter how broken: "The Spirit of the Sovereign Lord is on me, because the Lord has anointed me to preach good news to the poor. He has sent me to bind up the brokenhearted, to proclaim freedom for the captives and release from darkness for the prisoners . . . to comfort all who mourn, and provide for those who grieve in Zion- to bestow on them a crown of beauty instead of ashes, the oil of gladness instead of mourning and a garment of praise instead of a spirit of despair." Isaiah 61: 1-3b *NIV*

Jesus is the Healer and Deliverer of all our root problems, and His healing balm is His blood: "To Him who is able to keep you from falling and to present you before His glorious presence without fault and with great JOY!" Jude 1:24 *NIV*

What "root" in your life does God want to remove? The pain of removal cannot compare to the joy on the other side and the freedom from self-bondage.

THE FURNACE

There's a place no one discusses in polite company,
A sinister place of battling demons, where the fire is hotter and unholy.
A place of strap-down gurneys, glassless back
rooms with cots and padded walls,
Where the prisoners can be seen night and day
pacing up and down the confining halls.
The census is always maxed-out and the lines
for meds are familiarly long;
The staff is burnt-out to a crisp and doctors sing their shoveling song.
The docs write the daily orders, "More medicine, shovel it in!"
The nurses chart the progress notes so insurance
companies send more dollars to burn.
The month-long stay is abysmal; patients
overmedicated and trudging the halls,
Too out of their own mind to brush teeth or bathe,
some hitting the same old brick wall.
There's grandiose thinking, paranoia galore, and
hallucinations and violent behavior as well;
It's too bad these furnace workers can't send these
unholy demons straight back to hell.
Satan's alive and well in the furnace, and if your mind he can't dominate;
He'll just send a few of your furnace friends to
scorch you and leave you to your fiery fate.
Distorted, disordered thinking brought on
by stress; illicit drugs or plain life;
These are your ticket to the furnace, and believe
me, you'll pay the heavy price.
So read your Bible every day, pray, praise God
you're not where you've once been;
Our God is not a God of confusion, the result of Satan's selling sin.

"To whom much has been given, much will be required."
Luke 12:48 NIV

GIVING BACK

In the hit movie, "Pay It Forward," Kevin Spacey's character, a teacher, challenges his class with a year-long assignment of finding a way to change the world and implementing it.

Each of us has the ability to change the world, one person at a time, with the power of the Holy Spirit. And the Holy Spirit exponentially grows, according to our faith, to potentially reach millions for Jesus.

"To whom much has been given, much will be required." Giving back to others, or "Paying It Forward" ensures that we are not self-focused but other-focused, ministering to them.

If each day, we challenge ourselves to do at least one good deed for our fellowman in the name of Jesus, our day will have been productive, and God will bless our efforts.

We can read to the blind, teach someone to read, rake someone's yard, bake a friend cookies, visit an elderly person who may be lonely, pray with someone ill, make dinner for a stressed-out mom, clean house for a disabled person, take a neighbor to the store who doesn't have a car, sit with someone in the hospital, join a prison ministry or volunteer at a Christian church or organization. The list is endless!

Letting Go To Let God

We grasp so tightly at the reins of life, dead-sure that we're in control; we're convinced if we let go for a moment, our stagecoach downward will roll.

But life, like an unharnessed horse, is unpredictable and free, galloping full-on toward danger or cantering by the stream.

God is the Great Stagecoach Driver, and He's asking you for the reins; you've driven the horses long and hard — it's time to relinquish your domain!

You find it almost unbearable to let go and slowly climb in the coach; as the door swings shut, and He takes the lead, you really want to step out and approach. "Lord, isn't there a steep precipice up ahead? Aren't there bandits on this road?"

"Relax, my child, I'm in control. Quit carrying such a heavy load!"

As you sit back in the coach and shut your eyes, you begin to enjoy the ride. Your fears give way to faith as the Great Stagecoach Driver safely brings you aside.

When you reach your destination, though bumps and dangers filled the way, won't it be wonderful to see the Great Stagecoach Driver and hear Him say, "At my inn, won't you eternally stay?"

Myths of Mental Illness

There's a mighty-fine line of insanity that each of us are capable of crossing over,

Whether it's the bottle you can't let go of, or the dent in your 2016 high-end Range Rover.

Each of us obsesses, is in denial or emotionally stuffs something,

But most of us have hidden it well;

If the definition of insanity is doing the same thing over and over again, expecting different results, we each have our own little hells.

If keeping it all together and wearing a plastic smile works for you,

don't judge the rest of us for occasionally "losing it," acting out or coming unglued.

We all have our coping mechanisms for grief, loss, pain, and resentments that make us temporarily insane.

So the next time you spot the stereotypical madman, pushing a grocery cart or begging for change, remember your frailty and that it could be you if circumstances were rearranged.

DON'T GIVE UP

When the wreckage of your past threatens to steal your restfulness,
Remember He's thrown it all in the Sea of Forgetfulness. . . don't give up.
If some sudden course of events sends you reeling as if on a ship,
Remember that He holds the universe in His hands, and nothing will escape his grip . . . don't give up.
Though the waves about you billow, looming large and threatening be,
Just remember Jesus' command, "Be still!" and calmed the sea . . . don't give up.
When you've spent yourself completely and lost all hope of finding reward,
Remember He said, "Cast your nets on the other side,"
and the fishermen could barely keep the catch on board . . . don't give up.
We serve a God who parted waters, calmed seas, walked on water, and commanded the waves.
Is anything too difficult for Him? Don't give up!

THE SCHOOL OF SUFFERING

There's an Alma Mater that I dread, one whose lessons hurt heart and head, some assignments leave you wishing you were dead - - the school of suffering.

In some courses we enroll ourselves, creating chaos and mini-hells by not listening to life's warning bells- the school of suffering.

In graduate courses, we play victim of other's mistakes, scandalous, sanctimonious, proud, alternating with cruel hate, fighting believing with destiny, we had a date- the school of suffering.

How can we so audacious be, when our Lord Himself hung on a tree, learning obedience through His suffering-- the school of suffering?

For the joy set before Him, He endured the pain, the abandonment, scorn, and shame;

the wooden beams, the forsaking while He cried His Father's name-- the ultimate sacrificial suffering.

If we profess to follow Jesus Christ, He promised us suffering and sorrow in this life;

We must accept the lessons that have a price, for obedience often demands a sacrifice--in the school of suffering.

THE ONES WE FORGET

When Jesus said, " the least of these", I think He had in mind people who make us want to forget that frailty is of human kind.

There's Mary, who rocks back and forth, back and forth, in the smoke room all day long; rocking the baby she never had, comforting herself as she whispers a song.

There's Melvin, who has the strength of ten men, but the mentality of a 7-year-old; his father beat him with a frying pan when all he needed to do was to lovingly scold.

There's Roy-Gene, who'll tell you his two favorite kings are Jesus and the King of Rock-N-Roll; he was thrown from a car when his brother was driving drunk; his head trauma causes frustration untold.

There's sweet Jim, who has Cerebral Palsy, and he likes to talk and flirt; He's a 15-year-old in a 60- year-old body, twisted and gnarled, but complains not of hurt.

There's William, a frail man of 65, whose agoraphobia keeps him at the group home shut in; he listens to country music all day, content not to brag about where he's been.

There's Victoria, an 85-pound waif of a woman, her tongue as sharp as a knife; perhaps she acquired it living homeless on cold Chicago nights. Her babies were taken from her, and heart must have died that day. She's living now on oxygen, reunited to her family in a miraculous way.

Jesus said when we offer the least of these a listening ear, a smile, an embrace, a human act of kindness, we extend to them His grace.

And He said when we've done it to the least of these, we've, in essence, done it to Him.

There's a Jesus on the park bench, in the group home, at the prison gym. There's a Jesus in a jail cell, there's one waiting for a meal, there's a Jesus- the "least of these" —at your doorstep, Are you ready to help heal?

THE HUMAN COST OF SUFFERING

A silent scream, a lifeless body,
Face washed with tears
Bitter minutes ticking by
An anxious heart, rent with pain
Anguish in grotesque fears.
Distended bellies, disfigured limbs,
Muscles that shrink and atrophy.
Needle marks, gunshot wounds, bloodshot eyes
Prisoners waiting to be free.
Infanticide, suicide, homicide
Child abuse and neglect;
Prostitution, drive-bys, road rage
Gang members that demand respect.
Extortion, black market, automatic weapons
Rioting to bring about change;
Emotionless seas of faces in a
World filled with poignant pain.
Cancer, HIV, starvation
Nuclear escalation and catastrophe;
Oh, come quickly Lord Jesus and end our suffering.

BEAUTY FOR ASHES

Take these ashes, Lord,
The wasted years, months of mourning
Endless tears
Pain so tangible from rejection
That despair covers me
Like a shroud.
These are my grave clothes;
for years I was buried,
the weight of my Sin entombed me alive;
help me to shed them,
no longer bound-up by them,
Holy Spirit, open my eyes.
Help me to see the beauty for ashes
the Lord Jesus purchased for me;
in His death No grave could hold Him,
and in dying, He set me free.

LESSONS FROM A BUTTERFLY

From Zebra and Tiger Swallowtail, Painted Lady, royal
Monarch, and humble cabbage butterflies,
We learn life lessons --how quickly you grace the earth and die.
Your life is but a whisper, fleeing are your days on earth,
But complete transformation---metamorphosis
through you is what the Lord births.
Your caterpillar days behind you, the safe
cocoon which held you empty now,
Your amethyst and topaz wings ready to take flight,
A new creature miraculously, we still know not how.
Wafting with the wind, wavering high and low
through Rose of Sharon and butterfly bush,
Fragile wings are magnificently strengthened when
through life's difficulties they are pushed.
The dazzling, dizzying heights you fly to and the
colorful lantana to which you're drawn;
Drink deeply of this life's nectar, and savor every brand new dawn.
Spread joy like pollination, touching as many "flowers" as you go,
And reflect God's Son through your radiance
so His love for others shows.

DETOXIFICATION

I've been in countless rehabs, where the goal is to pull you through the
sweats, the shakes, the nausea and heartaches of the .23 you blew.
Staffs' eyes are ever upon you as you trudge from day to day, wondering
how you ever ended up in a bottle and if sober you'll truly stay.
But the pills, the diet, and the litany of
outpatient classes they'll recommend,
Can't compare with the detoxification process
that the Holy Spirit wants to begin.
One day the realization hits you that your drug
of choice was not the real bad guy,
But the symptom of a much worse malady;
It's self that is your problem and its cause is little old me.
Lord, only you can detoxify me of the dross that's in my life;
Only you can purify me from the pain and endless strife.
Lord, help me let go of all the ways I medicate,
vainly attempting to meet my needs;
Help me let go of toxic relationships that my self-sickness feeds.
Detoxify me in the furnace of your refiner's fire,
That self may be burned up and all-consumed with only your desire.

"My name is Legion for we are many." Mark 5:9 NIV

BATTLING THE WINDS AND WAVES TO HEAL ONE MAN

It had been a long day for Jesus and the disciples. Jesus spoke to the crowds in parables, as much as they could understand, and he was tired. That day when evening came, Jesus said to his followers, "let us go over to the other side (of the lake)" Mark 5:35 *NIV.* Leaving the crowd behind, they got in the boat, followed by other boats. A storm suddenly swept up, and the waves nearly capsized the vessel. Jesus, exhausted from the day's teaching, was sleeping in the stern.

"Teacher," said one of the disciples. "Don't you care if we drown?" Jesus quickly got up, rebuked the wind and said to the waves, "Quiet! Be still!" (v. 39 *NIV*). It was completely calm.

Not even the storm could keep Jesus from his destiny of meeting the demon-possessed man at Garasenes. The Bible says the no one was strong enough to subdue him, so he wandered among the tombs day and night, cutting himself with stones.

"When he saw Jesus from a distance, he ran and fell on his knees in front of him. He shouted at the top of his voice, "What do you want with me, Jesus, Son of the Most High God? Swear to God that you won't torture me" (v. 6-7 *NIV*). For Jesus had said to him, "Come out of this man, you evil spirit." Then Jesus asked him, "What is your name?"

"My name is Legion," he replied, "for we are many." But not too many demons for Jesus. When the townspeople came to see what had happened, the man was dressed and in his right mind.

If Jesus battled wind and waves to heal this one poor demoniac, how much more do you think He wants to free you?

NOTES

"I consider that our present sufferings are not worth comparing with the glory that will be revealed in us..." Romans 8:18 NIV

"Now if we are children, then we are heirs—heirs of God and co-heirs with Christ, if indeed we share in his sufferings in order that we may also share in his glory." —Romans 8:17 NIV

PRESENT SUFFERINGS FOR FUTURE GLORY

God's economy is so upside down from our own human standpoint. We frightened, frail humans will go to any lengths possible to avoid suffering; drugs to numb pain, physician-assisted suicide to end tragic life; alcohol in excess to wall us off from life's struggles; herion injections to feel euphoria, even if only briefly; putting off and avoiding pain of surgeries we know need; avoiding family members and close friends who have caused us pain. Is it any wonder the U.S. is known as the pill nation? We have the world's best medical care at our disposal, and yet we are one of the "sickest" nations in the world.

In the economy of God, according to Paul, "our present sufferings are not worth comparing with the glory that will be revealed in us" (Romans 8:18 *NIV*) This tells me that all those day I spent locked in the dungeon of despair, tempted to end my own life, will seem trivial when compared with the glory God will reveal in me! I imagine when we each reach heaven, the sufferings of this life will have a flip side, an upside-down logic that makes the glory ever more sweet.

Jesus, the Man of Sorrows, suffered unjustly at every turn, and yet in these verses in Romans 8:17 *NIV*, we are promised that our unjust sorrows allow us to share in His glory! When men revile you, speak ill of you, curse, you, ridicule you, label you as crazy, lazy, or stupid, mock you for taking the high moral ground, persecute you for being different, avoid you for acting strange, you have a glorious future to look forward to. With Jesus, you're in good company.

"But those who hope in the Lord will renew their strength. They will soar on wings like eagles; they will run and not grow weary, they will walk and not be faint." Isaiah 40:31 NIV

THE ONE TRUE HOPE-GIVER

Empty promises, dreams deferred, false hopes. All of these leave us feeling utterly hopeless, despondent, and depressed. We see and hear them everywhere in our culture; a pill that helps shed belly fat, a natural remedy that prevents colon cancer, a pillow that guarantees a better night's sleep, a mattress that keeps our partner from snoring, and a blender that helps us juice our way to health.

In all this clamoring for hope and empty promises, there is only ONE true hope-giver: the Lord, and He promises to renew our strength if we hope wholly on Him. While we trust that if we take our medications we will feel better, while we order our days to give our lives meaning, we feel more productive; while we interact with positive people who care for and love us, we cope better; but it is the Lord alone who gives us hope to renew our strength to face tomorrow.

When we are discouraged that our medicines aren't helping enough, when our days are not ordered in the way we had planned, when the people we love disappoint us, as they will, when life no longer seems worth living, when we think we'll never conquer all the ways we humans self-medicate, there is one who holds the universe in His hands. He wants to renew your strength daily, allow you to run and not grow weary, and walk through life's valleys without fearing evil. Hope in the one true Hope-Giver.

"If you return to the Almighty, you will be restored; If you remove wickedness far from your tent and assign your nuggets to the dust, your gold of Ophir to the rocks in the ravines, then the Almighty will be your gold, the choicest silver for you. Surely then you will find delight in the Almighty and will lift up your face to God. You will pray to him, and he will hear you, and you will fulfill your vows. What you decide on will be done, and light will shine on your ways. When men are brought low and you say, "Lift them up!" then he will save the downcast. He will deliver even one who is not innocent, who will be delivered through the cleanness of your hands."
Job 22:21-30 NIV

THE ALMIGHTY WILL
BE YOUR GOLD

What exactly is the "gold" in your life: the thing you value the most? Is it an illicit affair, a hobby of restoring expensive cars, a 401 K you've been faithfully contributing to, an expensive drug habit, endless gaming that robs you of precious time with love ones? A goal of making millions of dollars in real estate sales? Gambling on sports teams, keeping up with the Jones, getting ahead at work, no matter what the cost to your family?

In these verses, Eliphaz the Termanite reminds Job that God is the only true source of our "gold". If we are willing to assign our nuggets of gold to the dust, God Himself will be our most precious commodity, and the promises that follow make it well-worth the effort:

1) We will lift up our face to God and find delight in Him;

2) We will pray, and God will hear us;

3) You will fulfill your vows;

4) What you decide upon will be done (granted);

5) Light will shine on your ways;

6) When you say "lift up the downcast, it will be done;

7) And finally, He will deliver one who is not innocent through the cleanness of your hands.

I challenge you to lay aside the "gold" in your life and make the Almighty your gold. His promises never fail.

"I consider that our present sufferings are not worth comparing with the glory that will be revealed in us. The creation waits in eager expectation for the sons of God to be revealed. For the Creation was subjected to frustration, not by its own choice, but by the will of the one who subjected it, in hope that the creation itself will be liberated from its bondage to decay and brought into the glorious freedom of the children of God."
Romans 8:18-21 NIV

The Glory Revealed in Us

How different would be our perspective of suffering if we could catch but a small glimpse of the "glory that will be revealed in us"(v.18 *NIV*). Imagine if you can a child's leg braces thrown away, a pediatric cancer ward empty, a line of starving children in Ethiopia eating to their hearts' content, mourning families reunited with their deceased loved ones, violence, sin, death, and destruction no more.

These are but mere glimpses of that glory the whole creation groans for. The bondage of decay will be no more—only the "glorious freedom of the children of God." (v. 21 *NIV*)

Too often, I find myself stuck in the rut of self-pity for the suffering I'm enduring: hurtful words, the overwhelming tasks of the day, the dead weight of depression that cripples me, the negative voices in my head that must be overcome. . . but if I could just get a glimpse of God's glory that will be revealed in us, and the freedom of the children of God! Oh, what a difference that could make in my day. Pray that God would give you a glimpse of that glory today!